LOVE
OR DIE

*Finding oneness
in a me-first world*

Sandy Meadows
and
Stan Wenck, Ed.D.

First published by Dog Ear Publishing
4011 Vincennes Road
Indianapolis, IN 46268
www.dogearpublishing.net

ISBN: 978-145756-713-1

This book is printed on acid-free paper.
Printed in the United States of America

TABLE OF CONTENTS

FOREWORD

I n 1939, the poet W. H. Auden wrote, "We must love one another or die." Now authors Sandy Meadows and Stan Wenck reveal why Auden's wisdom is crucial, not only for personal psycho-spiritual growth but also for the survival of human culture and the human species. The love these authors elaborate is not the romantic, sappy Hollywood version, but love as the ultimate expression of the overcoming of separation and pathological, selfish individuality. Our country and our world are bleeding from various fault lines of separation — race, gender, religion, income inequality, environmental destruction, on and on. The disease of separateness now alienates us from other species and the earth itself. Emergency alarms are ringing. Will we listen? Novelist Alice Walker wrote: "Anything we love can be saved." But how to proceed? I can think of no better first step than heeding the wakeup message and gentle instruction in *Love or Die*. This splendid book deserves a national — nay, an international — audience. For all our sakes, I hope *Love or Die* is a best seller.

~ Larry Dossey, M.D.

Author: *One Mind: How Our Individual Mind Is Part of a Greater Consciousness and Why It Matters*

INTRODUCTION

Sometimes, it seems as though we Homo sapiens never learn from our mistakes. When we look at the history of human beings, we seem to endlessly repeat the same old prejudice, hatred, and divisiveness of the past and operate primarily in a me-first mode of consciousness. And so we wondered, are we ultimately doomed to self-destruction by our own inability to learn, grow, correct our mistakes, and evolve beyond them? Basically, we wanted to know: **What is preventing our evolution?** This is the question that weighs most heavily upon our consciousness.

At first, we looked only at some of the more superficial reasons why we might be unable to rise to higher levels of consciousness over the years, such as greed, ignorance, and narcissism. These factors are still very much a part of our landscape today, and many times we are totally unaware of their presence within our own psyche. But looking more deeply, we discovered two hidden **false beliefs** that are fully accepted and shared by almost everyone on the planet. And we realized how, if these false beliefs remained unchallenged by the wider populace, they would eventually lead to the destruction of civilization! They are keeping us trapped in an outmoded level of consciousness we call "the ego," and they are inhibiting the evolution of human beings.

The two false beliefs are actually very simple, but powerfully destructive: "**We are separate**," and "**We are incomplete**." One is a corollary of the other, and each belief is dependent upon the other. Together they stand, and together they must fall, because the truth is…

We are ONE and we are WHOLE.

PART I

LOVE'S TRANSFORMING POWER

Expanding our identity to include every segment of life

Chapter 1

EGO CONSCIOUSNESS: WHERE WE ARE NOW

Today, many people are stuck in a narrow and restrictive level of consciousness called "the ego." As cited in the introduction, they are stuck there primarily because they are unconsciously holding two **false beliefs** about themselves which, in all likelihood, have never been examined or questioned: 1) **We are separate;** and 2) **We are incomplete/broken/flawed.**

Let's investigate how we came to embody these beliefs. The ego level of consciousness initially evolved as a protective mechanism for the physical body. Like an animal instinct, we believed, "I am my body; therefore, I need to protect it." For purposes of this book, here is our working definition: "The ego is a limited sense of self that identifies exclusively with the physical body and brain, and so it sees itself as something *separate, imperfect,* and *defenseless* that needs to be protected – a finite thing apart from other finite things." The ego thus *prevents* us from recognizing our universal connectedness and interdependence with all forms of life. The ego cannot imagine that we are all *one*, because it so narrowly concentrates on its own "separate" physical body, trying to survive in a dangerous world.

The ego only thinks of the self as a glass half empty – where something is missing that needs to be filled. There is a subconscious belief that the self is somehow lacking and thus unworthy of love. So the ego seeks to augment and defend the self by constructing a stronger, more complete *self-image* of itself. It attempts to compensate for the underlying lack of self-love by creating a superficial public image of superiority and strength to reflect out into the world, as if that would somehow prove that it is whole and worthy of love. It may try to project an image of more money, more power, more intelligence, more athletic ability, more talent, better looks, and the like. But deep down, the need for self-love remains, and until that need is filled from *within*, in the form of genuine self-love, the ego will continue to look outward to fill the void with worldly symbols of success.

The consequence of this disconnect is that the ego defines the self as limited, finite, and incomplete. The ego identifies so completely with the "separate" physical body that it believes that's all it is – something temporary, flawed, and separate. Something broken. And it spends a lifetime trying to fix its brokenness in innumerable ways. It does not see its own wholeness.

Overlooked by the ego, within each and every one of us there is a Divine essence that is universal,

whole, and without needs. Some have called it our *spirit*. Others have called it *cosmic consciousness* or our *God-Self*. Whatever name you call it, this Divine essence has no fear, no insecurities, no needs, and no absence of love. When we give our Divine essence permission to express itself through our physical body, the ego will surrender its dominance, realign with its essential Self, and we will get a glimpse of true reality. We will begin to see how life can be when the ego is no longer in control. Our Divine essence is an ever-present reality, and it can show us the way forward if we will only embrace it and allow it expression.

Ego consciousness may have served to protect humans at one stage in our history, but it is now threatening to destroy humanity if we are not able to evolve beyond it. When carried to the extreme, those me-first ego-needs create greed, violence, craving for power and dominance – all for the enhancement of what we perceive as our small, separate ego-self. The ego's belief that we are separate and incomplete causes it to invent defense mechanisms to fill the needs we believe we have, and thus protect its fragile nature and perceived inadequacies. In this way, the ego tries to create the wholeness and the oneness that it believes it lacks, but it fails to recognize that the Self already HAS both wholeness and oneness – in its Divine essence!

It's a paradox: The ego creates a self-image that makes it *feel* more complete or even superior by covering up its insecurities. But since its underlying neediness always makes it think of itself first, there is a lack of genuine humility. On the other hand, the Divine Self doesn't need to be seen as more complete because it already *knows* its own wholeness. It has nothing to prove, and as a result the Divine Self has more humility than the ego self.

The purpose of this book is to urge you to discover your true Self – your Divine Self – and allow it to shine through to enlighten you. Allow it to help you evolve into a new level of being through the amazing power of love. A wonderful new level of consciousness awaits your discovery, and it is a place of infinite peace, joy, and harmony. No longer will you feel compelled to "fix" your life (or anyone else's). No longer will you be driven to compete to be top dog or most powerful leader, because the ego itself will become obsolete. You will KNOW beyond doubt your eternal worth, your essential wholeness. And you will realize you are *connected* with all that is.

To glimpse our universal oneness and wholeness is to comprehend that everything in existence is connected. Everything created is but an extension of your greater Self – your Divine essence – and therefore, ***if you harm another, you are only harming yourself.*** Conversely, ***if you harm yourself, you are harming another***. This knowledge is essential if we expect to evolve past the stagnant ego stage we are presently experiencing. If the ego is allowed to reign dominant, humanity will eventually destroy itself and the planet.

So, how do we begin to liberate our Divine Self from the constricted ego state we have created to define us? How do we find a more all-encompassing and authentic identity that is broad enough to embrace LOVE OF SELF? We begin by looking inward.

"There came a time when the risk to remain tight in the bud was more painful than the risk it took to blossom."

– Anaïs Nin

Chapter 2

LOVE OF SELF: THE STARTING POINT AND THE WAY FORWARD

To overcome the ego, self-love must come first. Love of self is the essential foundation for all other love. It is the opposite of egocentricity, which is not self-love at all, but a self-image based on need, fear, and protection.

Self-love is awareness and acceptance of your eternal value and worth exactly the way you are in your whole being.

But it's not enough just to say intellectually, "I am worthy; I am whole." It must be something you FEEL at the deepest level of your being. When it seems as if everyone else is against you, your sense of self-worth must be bulletproof. When it feels like no one else loves you, you must continue to love yourself and recognize your innate value – *and* the value of everyone else, particularly those who don't yet recognize their own value or yours. "Love your enemy" was no casual phrase when it was first spoken. It came from the very heart of the universe, and was directed to each and every one of us for all time.

Love of self cannot begin without first knowing yourself. Have you ever felt a lasting, authentic love for someone you didn't truly know? Probably not. And so it is with loving ourselves. Who are we really? How do we truly get to know ourselves? Let's begin with who and what we are not.

We are not our jobs and professions. Our conditioning society has shaped us to believe and value certain vocations and professions more highly than others. We then tend to categorize persons outside those professions at the lower end of the hierarchy. But that's not who we really are. We have infinite value regardless of what we do for a living.

We are not our possessions. Does a bigger house really make us bigger? Does a more elaborately equipped car guarantee to transport us unscathed through the hills and valleys of life? Can we "bank" on large monetary deposits to purchase emotional freedom or peace of mind? Or are these just status symbols that temporarily provide the illusion of "making it"? Have we, in fact, allowed our possessions to possess us?

We are not our race. We are not Caucasian, African-American, Asian, Latino, or Middle Eastern. Our essential Self is not defined by race, creed, nationality, or gender. We are all human beings, created equal in the sight of God. And we are so much more.

We are not our mistakes. Because we harbor the false belief that we are flawed and incomplete, we humans have a tendency to judge ourselves harshly for every mistake we make. Each mistake only further confirms our false belief, deepening the emptiness and the need within us for love of Self.

We are not our accomplishments. Because our true Self is whole and complete within itself, no number of achievements will ever make us any greater or more worthy than we already are. There is no need to try and perfect something that is already perfect. Our Divine essence has no need to seek accolades or glory. What material accomplishment could possibly be more exalted than divinity itself? Yet that is exactly what we are in our essence.

We are not our physical bodies. This one may be more difficult for you to accept, but it is true. Your body is the primary thing with which you identify. But consider this: Are you merely a physical body having a conscious experience? Or are you consciousness itself having a physical experience? Quantum physics is beginning to bear out the truth of the latter, as it maintains that everything in the universe is energy in the process of changing form. When you detach from the ego and make the shift from selfish to selfless, and when you become pure consciousness, you become simply an awareness in an infinite field of possibility. You're in the quantum field where all things are created. Look closely at the difference between a living body and a dead body; now find what is missing from the dead body that was present in the live body. Whether you call that missing element the "life force" or "spirit" or "consciousness," it is evident that the physical body alone is not who you really are.

Who are we then? Twenty-five hundred years ago, the Greek philosopher Socrates said, "The unexamined life is not worth living." He also said, "Know thyself." Four hundred years later, Jesus said, "You shall know the truth, and the truth shall set you free." He also said, "The kingdom of heaven is *within* you." These wise imperatives still await our response.

So, if we are not our physical bodies, or our possessions, accomplishments, or anything else, then how do we define what we *are*? If our formless life force or spirit or consciousness is not a material form, is it possible for us to reduce what is formless to a definition encapsulated in a word-form? The answer is: we can't. What is infinite can never be reduced to a finite definition. But here are a few things we *can* say about our Divine essence that can be verified experientially. *The truth that can set us free* is that:

- We have eternal worth and it is not something we have to earn.

- To know the truth is to experience our Divine Self within. Do not fear this experience; we are worthy of knowing the truth.

- The indivisible Whole is contained in each of the parts.

- Our infinite Spirit, our essence, is immortal, whole, complete, and perfect.

- Our Spirit can never be destroyed, but it can manifest in different forms.

- Our Divine Spirit is **one** with all that is – one with others, one with nature, one with the universe, and one with God.

- Our Spirit has NO NEEDS. Nada. Zip. NONE.

Research into "near-death experiences" has shed a great deal of light into the nature of consciousness and its relationship with the brain. NDEs, as they are called, indicate that we can have conscious experiences *outside* of our physical body. They provide scientific evidence that there is a fundamental underlying reality at the core of life that is spiritual in nature. This spiritual reality appears to be able to function even when the brain has flat-lined! Whether we are aware of it or not, we all participate in this Divine essence, which has unconditional love as its core principle. This *cosmic consciousness* in which we are immersed is pervasive throughout space and time, and it is the next level of consciousness in our evolution. To fully activate its awesome powers, we need only open ourselves to its presence, which is already within us.

The consequences of continuing to accept the two false beliefs created by the ego will be tragic. If we persist in believing we are each a *separate* and *flawed* piece of a large disconnected puzzle in a random and chaotic universe, we are constantly going to be living on the edge. The stress levels will be unbearable as we try to fend for ourselves, believing we are a small and insignificant speck of eternity, scratching and clawing to eke out a brief existence and then to perish forever. That is, if we focus **only** on our material body and believe it is the ***entirety*** of our being, stress and worse will inevitably be our fate.

With our budding awareness of our Divine essence comes the realization that we are not a *separate* physical being as we have been conditioned to believe. We are part of a formless, eternal reality that is whole, complete, and perfect. It creates, animates, and sustains all the created forms in the universe, including humans. To experience our oneness with this universal reality is to experience our *cosmic identity*, our God-consciousness. It is to attain knowledge of our connection with infinite Being. And the more we allow our Divine Self to have expression through our physical body, our mind, and our feelings, the happier our life will become. Moving out of ego consciousness and into a higher level of consciousness is an amazing stress reliever! Try giving yourself this gift of love.

"You yourself, as much as anybody in the entire universe, deserve your love and affection."

– Buddha

In the following chapters, let's set out to discover our very real connection with every segment of life. Remember, we are not incomplete and we are not separate. **We are WHOLE and we are ONE.**

Chapter 3

LOVE OF FAMILY

As a tiny, helpless embryo, we are physically connected to our mother in the womb. After we are born, are we not still connected with her in some way? Physically, as she brings comfort, food, and warmth to us? Mentally, as she challenges our growing minds? Emotionally, as she soothes our hurts and fears? Consciously, through an unseen awareness that connects the two of you? Could we survive on our own without our connection to her?

In childhood, as we gradually move into a broader awareness of the world around us, one of the first things we learn is acceptance of differences. We witness the interactive give-and-take of other family members, as they support each other in the business of survival. Parents (or parent figures) take care of our bodily needs; they feed us; they provide us with food, clothing, and shelter; they help us keep clean; and they teach us life skills we will need to survive on our own. At some point, there is a recognition on our part that their gift of giving is an expression of their love for us. We *feel* it. And in gratitude for their gift, we express our love for them in return. In our mutual sharing, cooperation, and caring, the Divine love that we *are* is made manifest and expresses itself through our corporeal being.

As our awareness grows, we see that each member of our family is also a unique individual who has a different appearance, different personality, different ideas, and different needs from our own. Yet we feel a *connection* with them as a necessary and cherished member of our immediate family, and so we learn tolerance of the differences between us. We need each other, in spite of differences, so we learn how to respect our differences. Acceptance, tolerance, and respect are all aspects of love.

Slowly, almost imperceptibly, our identity begins to expand from a very narrow focus on our own needs to an inclusion of the needs of others in our family. Instead of concentrating solely on what our ego wants at any given moment, our identity grows to a point where we begin to care about the wants and needs of our siblings, our parents, and others in our extended family. This is the first baby step to becoming a citizen of the world. We move from believing "I am my ego-self" to believing "I am an integral part of my family." It is a natural part of the maturation process for our *identity* – **our sense of who we really are** – to continue to expand throughout our lives.

What happens when something interrupts that process and inhibits the growth of our awareness and thus our identity? This is an important question that begs to be answered, because it is where so many in our culture find themselves today.

There are serious consequences if we halt the expansion of our awareness and our loving connection with each and every segment of life, and they all relate to quality-of-life issues: physical, emotional, mental, and spiritual. If we remain in an arrested state of separation and allow the ego to have full authority over our being, the result will be suffering for the individual as well as the entire planet. There will be dysfunction within families and communities. There will be disharmony and unrest between people and between nations. High stress levels will promote an increase in things like opioid addiction, crime, and suicide. But all of this can be avoided if we allow the natural expansion of our awareness and our intimate identification with every form of life to unfold.

> *"He who experiences the unity of life sees his own Self in all beings, and all beings in his own Self."*
> **– Buddha**

Let's explore other segments of life with which we might interact and extend our love.

Chapter 4

LOVE OF ANIMALS

Can you remember your first puppy or kitten? It was easy to fall in love with that little ball of fur because it gave us unconditional love and wanted nothing more than to be cuddled and loved by us in return. We felt an instant closeness and oneness with our pets, and began to connect with all other animal species as a result of that initial experience.

Before the advent of cars and trains, animals were much more than just beloved companions. They were our means of transportation. Horses, mules, camels, and elephants all helped us to reach places we wanted to go, and also helped us to move heavy objects we could not lift.

For some of our distant ancestors, animals and birds were the only source of food. Later, domesticated animals such as goats and cows provided milk and cheese for growing youngsters. It is safe to say that during the early stages of our evolution, we could not have survived without animals. We depended upon them for our very survival. Cave drawings show that early man had a reverence for animals, and some animals were worshiped in early forms of religion. Primitive man felt a sacred connection with the animals upon which they were dependent. Some even dressed up like these animals during holy rituals.

Consider the awe, adoration, and love extended by children to the amazing animals at a zoo or aquarium. Can we doubt that a dolphin has a soul? As some of life's most endearing creatures, animals afford us a wonderful vehicle to develop a growing appreciation of our magnificent natural world.

Throughout human history, our connection with animals has been deep, so our identity continued to expand. Our sense of what comprised our family circle came to include our beloved animals. Instead of caring only about the well-being of ourselves and our closest family members, we began to love and care about the well-being of our animals. Our "family" continued to enlarge as other species became incorporated into our identity.

"The greatness of a nation and its moral progress can be judged by the way its animals are treated."
– Mahatma Gandhi

Chapter 5

LOVE OF NATURE

We take many essentials from our beloved trees and plants in the form of food, shelter, and even the very air we breathe. If we love and appreciate their contribution to our welfare, it is not only our responsibility, but our mark of respect to give back to them in return – for their preservation and our mutual evolution. We are inextricably intertwined.

Nature is absolutely indispensable to our survival, yet we sometimes forget our connection with it. Early Native Americans felt a deep bond with the earth and all its creatures. They experienced a sacred oneness with and dependence upon Mother Earth, sensing that *all* life forms have some level of awareness that connects them with each other. They knew, and still know, that all life is precious.

It is never too late for us to reconnect with nature. Because we are part of nature, it gently nudges us back into a remembrance of love. Nature is authentic, never pretentious. Let us allow nature to guide us back to the Divine within us by making time to regularly visit a state or national park. Pause to savor some segment of nature's bounty: the beauty of a refreshing rainfall, the staccato of raindrops on windowpane and roof, cascading streams and rivulets, soft rumbles in the distance, forests rustling, animals scurrying. Experience now, with all of nature, one of life's wondrous lullabies. We are *one* with nature.

The parable of the tree

Try to think of a tree floating in space, existing as a thing separate from all other things. It's difficult to imagine because a tree can't exist in a vacuum. It needs many other things to keep it alive, such as soil, sun, wind, rain, insects, fungi, and so on. A tree cannot exist separately from all these other essential elements. The tree, the soil, the sun, the rain – all are connected in one working ecosystem. They are part of an organic whole whose elements are interconnected and interdependent for their mutual survival. They nourish each other to maintain a perfect balance of nature, and without that cooperation, that give-and-take, they would die. The same is true for humans; we cannot and do not exist as an entity separated from nature. We are part of that same ecosystem, for we, too, need all of the same elements for our survival that are needed by nature. We are one with nature.

Take a moment to think about the oxygen in our atmosphere, manufactured by the trees, and how absolutely essential it is for human life. Now contemplate the consequences if all the trees in the rain forests were harvested. Consider ways that renewable clean energy sources such as solar and wind power might contribute to retaining the balance of nature. What are some of the ways we can be more responsible stewards of Earth's precious resources needed for our survival?

> *"No man is an island, entire of itself."*
>
> **– John Donne**

Chapter 6

LOVE OF INSTITUTIONS

Humans are by nature gregarious. We want and need to belong. Following membership in our most longstanding primary group – the family structure – many of us then seek out affiliations within our various peer groups which bring us together with others of mutual interests, skills, and goals. Many different organizations have been developed to enhance our sense of completion and connection with others. Let's take a look at some of them.

Loving our schools. After home upbringing, our schools become the most influential societal element impacting the lives of our future citizens. But they *cannot* do their best work in isolation. Interaction between parents, schools, and communities consistently produces the most favorable results for all participants. Students whose parents are involved with their schools and educational processes are more likely to attend more regularly, earn higher grades, have higher rates of graduation and college attendance, and demonstrate higher self-esteem. Added benefits occur when schools, in turn, provide opportunities for improving parental skills and child-rearing knowledge.

Loving our place of worship. Ideally, our place of worship offers us a setting in which we can truly be who we are. For many, our place of worship can become a haven of safety where we are able to drop our mask and "come out of hiding" – a place where we can accept ourselves as *whole* and *complete.* The joyful result is an expanding connection with all we encounter. Our church then becomes a place which fosters both *realness* and *healing.* Who could not love a church like that?

However, it is important that we do not primarily identify our church as a brick-and-mortar building where we gather once a week, or a fixed set of belief systems that we must accept in total. Our church is a spiritual dimension of depth *within us,* all of us, wherever we are, seven days a week, twenty-four hours a day.

Loving our workplace. No institution is in greater need of a liberating sense of self-completion and connection than our workplace. A higher percentage of the population than ever before is now in the workplace, with more women functioning either as principal breadwinners or dual earners. People spend one-third of their adult lives on the job. The workplace is the center of a nation's economy with its special concerns of productivity, quality, and competition.

Workplace environments which promote awareness of one's feelings, open communication, and humanitarian goals over strictly profit motives tend to produce the happiest employees and those who exhibit the greatest job satisfaction.

Loving our sports teams. Each year, countless spectators watch and attend sports contests at all levels of competition to share in the passion that surrounds the athletes and their unique world. Just anticipating these events fires our emotions! Studies show that being identified with a favorite team may be just as important to us as our work, social, or even religious groups. What is it about sports that so captivates us? Let's examine this in some detail.

We spectators project our own hopes and aspirations onto the players on the fields and in the coliseums. We feel a measure of kinship and camaraderie with others who share our enthusiasm. More importantly, few human activities provide an arena in which superbly integrated *teamwork* and *connection* are so vividly portrayed. The old adage that there is no "I" in "team" was never so true. Individual egos must be left on the bench for group success. Differences in age, race, and culture become unimportant. The great player exhibits a type of wholeness and completeness that is emulated by teammates. All of this electrifies our desire for togetherness, communion, and connection with others. No wonder we want more!

Sports, then, provides a unique opportunity to take us out of our ego-self and into a wider level of identity in which we are all pursuing common goals with persistence, dedication, and joy. It allows us to participate in a cause greater than ourselves.

The same may also be said for work, worship, social groups, and the arts. They, too, take us out of our narrow self-interests and into an awareness of larger group goals. As our various relationships expand, so does our identification with the wide variety of organizations we derive pleasure and benefit from.

> *"If everyone is moving forward together, then success takes care of itself."*
>
> **– Henry Ford**

Chapter 7

LOVE OF COMMUNITY

A community is a basic social unit whose inhabitants reside in a specific locality and share a common government and cultural practice. Each of its diverse and talented members is uniquely necessary for the survival and well-being of the whole community.

A few of these members stand out as community leaders in their given field, and we are particularly indebted to them for their countless contributions to our welfare and advancement. These are the people who willingly assume responsibility for sharing their depth of knowledge with others. They impart their Divine Self into the community as a whole. We can learn much from each of them.

Who has not had a gifted teacher who impacted their life? These educators exhibit selfless caring and interest in their students. As a result of their personal integrity, they teach us values as much as subject matter. They serve as surrogate parents. **They love themselves (but not egocentrically), and they love what they do.** Their loving influence can last for generations. And each fortunate pupil likewise influences others, making a teacher's "touch" upon humanity exponentially valuable.

Our police and firefighters put themselves in harm's way on a daily basis for our safety. Their selfless service to others reveals their deep sense of connection to their community. One could even assume that their desire for a whole and undamaged community is inspired by their own sense of wholeness. These are true community heroes.

Dedicated nurses and physicians who go "above and beyond the call of duty" to eradicate disease and discomfort deserve mention as well. The extra time and devotion they spend with patients pays dividends in terms of reduced healing time and faster cures. Where does this devotion come from? It derives from an inner love of being of service.

We depend upon farmers and growers for the most basic of our needs – the production of sufficient food for our bodies. They are entrusted with the cultivation and care of the soil that will provide for our increasingly populous communities. Their loving concern for Mother Earth merits our deepest appreciation.

Finally, we owe a debt of gratitude to those individuals who provide us with the priceless beauty of the arts, whether in visual, musical, or literary form. These contributions give voice to our emotions. They are calming, uplifting, and they connect us in magical ways. They are concrete manifestations of the *divinity* within us. As such, they add to the enrichment and enjoyment of every resident.

Each member of our community contributes his unique part to the greater good. We are intimately connected with our community, and we are dependent upon it for our survival.

> *"Each of us dwells in a cathedral of our own Being that is created vast enough to encompass Unity with all creation."*
> **– Jonathan Lockwood Huie**

Chapter 8

LOVE OF COUNTRY

Most of us feel a rush of national pride when we hear our national anthem played or see our flag unfurl. But what does love of country really mean? Is it blind loyalty? Is it a belief that our own country always does the right thing, or that it is superior to other nations? Patriotism swells up from a sense of belonging and deep connection – not from feelings of exclusion or superiority.

It is possible for us to have a strong national identity without rejecting other countries. It is also possible to have a loving concern for our own country *and* a desire to continuously improve its systems and efficiencies. Love of country, like love of family, is demonstrated by participation, dedication, and conscious support.

We will not always agree with every political decision that our government makes. But we must remain dedicated to the give-and-take of a fair and democratic process, and we must get involved in that process. Our participation – our equal voice – is an essential contribution to the well-being of our nation as a whole. We want the best for our country; we want it to be healthy and harmonious; so our participation is actually a way of showing our love.

Even within a democracy, there are different concepts of "freedom." Some view freedom as the right to acquire wealth without government restrictions, while others passionately feel that freedom requires responsibility, including governmental safeguards of economic security and respect for marginalized groups.

Now and then, ego needs become apparent in the ruthless way some pursue their personal ambitions. Sometimes, we feel it when people around us are forcefully expending energy defending "our way" as opposed to "their way." But these instances are only temporary diversions from the straight and narrow path to compassionate, *universal* goals. Eventually, if we are truly all one, we will begin looking toward the good of the *whole* country, rather than just the betterment of a few privileged individuals. If we genuinely love our country and respect all of its citizens, we will protect the rights of everyone and value our democratic principles more than selfish or narrow-minded partisanship.

Knowing we are all one, we will find a way. United we will stand – divided we will fall.

Perhaps we should also mention the sense of pride we feel for the awesome natural beauty of our country. Majestic mountains, endless blue skies, forests teeming with wildlife, lakes and rivers – all offer us pure enjoyment and deep emotional refuge from the cares of everyday life. But remember, if we truly love our children and our grandchildren, we will protect and preserve that land, air, and water for the benefit of future generations.

True love of country must stem from the heart. More specifically, from hearts which are whole and complete within themselves and keep an open and altruistic connection with others. Complete and well-connected communities result from hearts such as these, which in turn spawn the greatest nations of the earth.

A few possible ways to show our love for our country: **vote**; volunteer as a mentor for at-risk youth; support equal pay for equal work; aspire to membership on county councils; start an organization in which we can manifest our unique talents in service to others.

"The love of one's country is a splendid thing. But why should love stop at the border?"

– Pablo Casals

Chapter 9

LOVE OF PEOPLE WHO ARE DIFFERENT

"A people without knowledge of their past history, origin, and culture is like a tree without roots."

– Marcus Garvey

Let's take time out to do a little self-reflection here. Think about how your life has been conditioned by the environment you grew up in: your family; its customs and beliefs; your friends and their influence upon you; your neighborhood environment; your regional climate; your educational opportunities; your religious training; your choice of vocation; your choice of spouse; on and on.

How much of your early environment played a role in who you turned out to be? Did you follow in your father's profession? Your mother's religion? Do your speech patterns reflect the neighborhood you grew up in? If we are completely honest with ourselves, we will quickly realize how much we were influenced (whether positively or negatively) by the customs and traditions of our immediate culture. Our surroundings shaped who we are today.

Now, stretch your imagination for a moment. Imagine how your life might be different today if you had been born into a totally different family, with different customs and beliefs, in another part of the world, with a totally different climate, other educational opportunities and religious training, and completely different choices for a vocation or a spouse. Is it possible that you would have turned out the same as you are now? Might you in fact be a totally different person with different ideas and experiences than you presently have? Be completely honest. Now, answer this: Could you (the person you are today) *accept* yourself as the person you have imagined from another culture? Could you *respect* that person? Could you *love* that person?

Here is the takeaway. You could *be* that person. It was only an accident of birthplace that shaped who you are today. Would you want people to hate you or discriminate against you if you indeed *had* been born into another culture? Look deeply. Do you have a judgmental attitude toward those who look different or have different beliefs and customs from yours? Take the time to put yourself in another person's shoes whenever you experience fear or rejection of those who are different from you. They may in fact be experiencing the same emotions toward you! Try to feel a kinship with the whole human race, of which you are a part. Learn to appreciate the many scientific and humanitarian contributions by those who are different. ***Love your "neighbor" as yourself.***

We are all a product of our culture. That's what makes each of us unique. Every single one of us has one-of-a-kind value and is capable of making a matchless contribution to the world. But underneath our talents and our culture and our conditioning, we are all the same. Underneath, we are one in Spirit. We share in a universal God-consciousness.

"He who is devoid of the power to forgive is devoid of the power to love."

– Martin Luther King, Jr.

Chapter 10

LOVE OF COUNTRIES THAT ARE DIFFERENT

Chapter 10 begins where Chapter 9 left off. It is only one small step from a different culture to a different country, so let's get right at it. Have you ever been conditioned during your life to believe that your country has "enemies"? Do any of your friends or family members "hate" other nations because they are "different"? Do you? This may take some soul searching, especially if you have never even met someone from the "other" group or made an effort to understand them.

We are *all* different in some way. Built into the nature of life is the fact that we need diverse experiences from which to learn. Think how many times an apparent obstacle in your life yielded a new lesson and became a blessing in disguise.

To reframe your views regarding "allies" versus "adversaries," consider the following:

1. Focus upon the Divine essence within another, rather than his words or behavior.

2. Try to understand how that person might have developed his or her beliefs.

3. Appreciate the richness and beauty in the diversity of other traditions.

4. Remember that we are all One. Separation is an illusion.

5. Adopt a continuous attitude of forgiveness. Even if it doesn't change another's behavior, forgive for your own sake. Release, detach, and bless them on their way.

6. Adopt an attitude of gratitude for any and all lessons learned.

Focusing on your Divine essence, and that of others, gives you the rock-solid stability you need to withstand the shifting winds of judgment dispensed by your ego. That way, if your ego is bruised by someone, your immediate reaction will not be a loss of self-esteem or an urge to retaliate.

Your Divine essence is like the eye of the hurricane – when chaos is swirling around you, your center will be completely calm and composed within itself. The same is true if someone flatters you. Your ego's immediate reaction would be an *elevation* in self-esteem. But when you ride the ego roller coaster, your self-esteem will be at the mercy of all the ups and downs of compliments and criticisms. Only your Divine essence has the necessary stability to weather both extremes. Your Divine Self doesn't need to be seen as attractive or intelligent or talented or powerful. Your Divine Self is *already* completely whole and without needs. Your Divine Self is equal to and one with every other being.

We are all connected in cosmic consciousness, and our collective fate rests upon each other! War is a primitive and barbaric way to solve problems in a civilized world. We have the power to create war or to create peace. It is our choice. But if we don't cooperate, we will NOT survive. We're all in this together. Will we evolve or will we perish?

"Destiny is not a matter of chance; it is a matter of choice; it is not a thing to be waited for; it is a thing to be achieved."
– William Jennings Bryan

"No culture can survive if it attempts to be exclusive."
– Mahatma Gandhi

*"Separate identity is an illusion. There are no **others**; we are all part of the same whole. We need a return to wholeness through love. Love is the only power that can save us."*
– Ervin Laszlo

The parable of the beautiful hand.

Imagine that each part of your body could FORGET that it was connected to all the other parts. So, instead of working together for the good of the whole, each part of your body only worked for itself and saw itself as a separate entity. Just suppose that your hand, for example, cared nothing about the rest of your body and began taking more and more precious nutrients away from the other parts of your body and keeping them for itself. Pretty soon, the hand would begin to look richer and more luxurious than the other body parts, and vanity would begin to play an even bigger role. With little regard for the rest, the hand begins to take even more nutrients from the other parts. The more beautiful the hand becomes, the more the other parts wither and grow weak and depleted of vital energy and nutrition. Yet the hand is so completely self-absorbed that it fails to notice anything but its own beauty. One day, the entire body dies – the beautiful hand along with it.

Moral of the story: We are not separate; we are all ONE.

Think about how a self-image of separation or superiority could ultimately contribute to a person's downfall. What might happen if we were all uncaring or even unconscious of the needs of others? Take a few minutes to consider your beliefs about who and what you are. What is your sense of self? Do you see yourself as part of a larger whole? Or do you see yourself as an island unto itself? Have you absorbed fierce competition and survival of the fittest philosophies into your attitudes required for a successful life? Do you feel any empathy toward or any responsibility for the welfare of other beings or the environment? Do you feel an intimate connection with planet Earth, or is it something to be exploited or polluted for personal gain? These are tough questions that deserve to be answered. Write down what you've discovered.

"The only thing that will redeem mankind is cooperation."
– Bertrand Russell

Chapter 11

LOVE OF THE EARTH

Try now to perceive the earth as a living organism. The rivers and the streams function like the arteries and the capillaries in our bodies. They carry life-giving water to distant parts of the globe, just as blood is circulated throughout our bodies. Where there are parched and cracked patches of dry soil, we can imagine them to be the wrinkles on the old face of Earth. Where there are young seedlings sprouting, view them as the nurturing maternal instincts of the planet at work. We ourselves are nourished by the fruits of Mother Earth, and could not exist without her generous and abundant offerings. In many ways, we are a microcosm of the planet, just as an atom is a microcosm of our solar system. There is a beautiful symmetry in the harmony of the heavens and the earth.

We feel a certain sense of awe and reverence whenever we witness the grandeur of the oceans, the majesty of the mountains, the power of a volcano, or the magnificence of the Grand Canyon. It is both humbling and inspiring to take in the beauty of our planet, and we can't help but feel gratitude for being a part of Earth's totality. It is easy to understand why Native Americans feel a deep connection with the earth. It takes little effort to love the earth, to feel a familial identity with it and a desire to protect it. In a very real sense, the earth gave birth and life to us, and we are an integral part of its family.

Recently, there was a news report that the Whanganui River in New Zealand had been granted legal status as a "human," with all the rights and protections a human would have. The river is considered sacred by the local Maori tribe, and it can no longer be polluted in any way. It must be treated as a "living entity." Tribe spokesman Gerrard Albert said, "We consider the river an ancestor; … from our perspective, treating the river as a living entity is the correct way to approach it, as an *indivisible whole…*" The new status of the river means if someone abused it or harmed it, the law now sees no differentiation between harming the tribe and harming the river, because they are *one and the same*. The passage of this law has taken 140 years of negotiation, the longest-running litigation in New Zealand's history. The river now has its own legal identity with corresponding rights.

Shortly thereafter, two other rivers in India – the Ganges and the Yamuna – were granted the same rights and legal protections. It was heartening to realize that some governments had progressed to such an extent that they now recognized, loved, and revered the rivers for the life-giving power they possess and their unity with the rest of life.

These testimonies are evidence of the mounting efforts to raise our consciousness to an awareness of the *sacredness of all life*. Perhaps one day we can look forward to a world in which all of life is treated with such reverence.

"There are no passengers on Spaceship Earth. We are all crew."
– Marshall McLuhan

Chapter 12

LOVE OF THE UNIVERSE

Our universe is a single living organism. It is, by definition, all of time, space, and its contents. It includes planets, suns, moons, stars, galaxies, the air we breathe, and all matter and energy. Our universe is comprised of every element we need to survive as a fully functioning part of the whole. It is literally everything in creation, including us. And just as every cell in our body is alive, so too are all the parts of the universe alive.

The *One Infinite Life Force* that creates, animates, and sustains our universe also constitutes its very *Being*.

Try to think of the universe as having a "soul" or "spirit." In other words, Being (the invisible life force we call God) is not *separate* from the physical universe. In fact, there is nothing apart from the Infinite Life Force. God/Spirit/Being is expressing *as* a universal organism, of which we are a functioning part. That means that Infinite (non-physical) Being has become a universal physical thing, but is not in any way limited by its materiality. (Refer to Chapter 13 for a more detailed explanation of this.)

The universe is the macrocosm that is reflected within every microcosmic part of itself, down to the subatomic level. It embraces everything that exists, everything that has existed, and everything that will exist. It encompasses all of life and all of history. Each one of us, as a complete being, is connected to it and part of it. Can you imagine that our universe – said to be some 13.8 billion years old – is still expanding both materially and energetically? Do we fully appreciate that our own individual expansion is not only an integral part, but a driving force of this evolution? Our universe is an awesome aggregate of all that is!

Infinite Being, manifesting as our universe, wraps us in its unconditional love – exactly as we are. It pays no heed to perceived flaws or misdeeds. It does not judge us to be anything less than holy. It accepts us as perfect and Divine expressions of itself. It sees its own wholeness and perfection reflected within us, because we are a part of the Whole. To ascend to a full awareness of and a participation in this universal love, we must rise above our societal notions that we need certain material things, accomplishments, or admiration in order to prove our worth. These are false beliefs.

How often do you entertain thoughts of deficiency? Do they have to do with amassing more and more material things? Can you slow down, relax, and become more receptive to the radiant love of our universe? Do you practice thoughts of appreciating and fully accepting yourself? Can you stop seeking love, acceptance, and approval from the outer world, and know that all the love you seek is fully within you? As you spend more and more time tuning in to the loving presence of your higher Self, you will gradually realize that you are actually tuning in to the universal Source of love. Too much time spent planning, achieving, or focusing on what we "lack" gets us out of tune. Regular meditation can reduce worldly cravings and create the receptivity needed to get us back "home" to the natural rhythms of our beloved universe.

Surrender now to the love and joy that is within you, and trust in the love of universal Being, to which you are connected. That love has always been there and will always be there. It is who you *are*.

Mother Earth, our celestial home in the universe, exists in perfect relationship with our solar system and galaxy to support life here. *Home* means something far deeper than just a physical dwelling. Some have said that home is where the heart is. That would suggest that home is not a place but a state of mind. It is a feeling of perfect comfort and peace that emanates from deep within our Divine spirit, and sometimes also from within a group of like-minded individuals who are able to freely express their inner spirit and share their feelings of connectedness with others.

This "paradise within" has the capacity to sweep away all feelings of separation and incompleteness, and produce continuous joy. Thus, when you are *home*, you feel a deep inner sense of belonging, no matter where you are. You sense being an essential part of the entire universe. You recognize beyond doubt your own wholeness. You feel connected with every living thing and with all that is sacred. You experience your own divinity.

This inner "home" can be nurtured and maintained at all times by remembering these two fundamental truths: **We are whole. And we are one.** Make this your life's affirmation and prayer. As the Desiderata says, "You are a child of the universe, no less than the trees and the stars; you have a right to be here." Our universe is an organic unity – a whole. Allow yourself to feel *at home* in the oneness of Life.

The ever-present and ever-abundant love that is continuously streaming from our universe prompts the question, "How do we experience, express, and return that love more fully?"

Consider the following:

- Start each day with an attitude of gratitude.

- Begin a practice of meditation and give your mind some time off.

- Send some love to people you know – and some you don't.

- Be forgiving of yourself and note your progress going forward.

- Surrender your "plan" at intervals and let life take over.

- Love yourself just as you are.

- Take a walk in nature: appreciate the beauty of flowers and sky; listen to the birds' songs; smell the grass and feel the wind.

- Practice loving yourself and others until you get good at it.

Step into your cosmic identity!

"The cosmos is within us. We are made of star-stuff. We are a way for the universe to know itself."

– Carl Sagan

"Love is possible only when there is a deep acceptance of oneself, the others, the world. Acceptance creates the milieu in which love grows, the soil in which love blooms."

– Osho

Chapter 13

LOVE OF THE ONENESS AND WHOLENESS WE ALL SHARE

Every finite form has boundaries and limitations in space and time;
The formless Infinite has no boundaries or limitations.

- How do you conceive the Divine? As finite or infinite?

- Do you believe that what we call "God" is omnipotent (all-powerful), omniscient (all-knowing), omnipresent (present everywhere), and eternal (in all time)?

- Do you believe you are a finite being, separate from others and from the Divine?

If you believe you are separate from God, then God cannot be all-knowing, all-powerful, all-present, or eternal. If the Divine is separate from us, then it is just another THING, alongside other things. And since all things have limitations (a beginning and an end in space and time), a separate God would be reduced to a finite form.

Some philosophers and theologians (Paul Tillich comes to mind) make a distinction between God as "**a being**" versus God as "**BEING**" itself. If you are familiar with the work of Eckhart Tolle, this is similar to his distinction between "form" and "formless."

"BEING" is a word used to describe the formless, infinite life force or energy throughout the entire universe. "A being" describes an individual, finite manifestation of that life force. A being is created, animated, and sustained by BEING itself. A being is one of the many ways formless BEING expresses itself in form. There are many different beings created out of the one life force, but they are not *separate* from that life force. These beings are all contained *within* BEING itself.

It's a paradox: The One becomes the many without ever losing its oneness! The One infinite life force is not separate from the many created beings. What is infinite can *never* be separate from what is finite; if it were separate, it would not be infinite. So, if you believe God is infinite, you must also believe that all of creation is one with God.

The reason so many of us are reluctant to believe we are one with God is because our ego does not want to give up the idea that we are separate. Since the ego identifies exclusively with form, it is unable to believe that we are connected with God or with each other in any way. The ego likes to believe it is separate and special and either superior or inferior to other beings. It wants to believe in form because form can be seen, and it fears the formless because it's afraid it's not real. The ego is a prisoner of its own fear. What the ego doesn't yet realize is that its desire to be *separate* is also a desire to be limited, because all *things* are limited.

To live as a form (i.e., a being) is to live as a temporary structure with limitations. To repeat: **To live as a form is to live with limitations.** If you want to experience limitations and come into Being as a (human) form, that is your choice and there's nothing wrong with it. It's okay to become a form and experience the limitations of that form. However, if you want to return to the Source, you cease to live as a so-called "separate" form and return home to your natural formless and unbounded state of BEING. (Fear will generally keep you bound in form.J)

But, ironically, **knowing this truth will permit you to live fearlessly IN form here and now**! (You have never left your formless state!) So, either way, you can live joyfully and peacefully. This knowledge is "heaven on Earth." *This* is the truth that will set you free. Once you surrender and completely accept the fact that while you are experiencing life *through form*, you will experience all the limitations that come with life in that form. So, sit back and enjoy the ride!

You always have been and you always will be connected with God (your universal Divine essence – your cosmic identity – your God-Self), in spite of any appearance to the contrary. That knowledge is your ultimate source of comfort and peace. If, however, you are still identifying with an ego-image you have created about yourself, or have feelings of unworthiness and still believe you are *separate* from God, then you may be failing to fully love yourself and recognize your beautiful deeper nature within. If you look only on the surface, your body does appear to be a finite form, separated from other forms. But that is just a trick of our five senses and our limited understanding of the Infinite. **If the Infinite is real, then it cannot be other than all-inclusive.**

The Infinite is a universal life force / energy / intelligence / consciousness – and NOTHING is separate from it, because all finite forms are created by and contained within this Source field. You are part of that Source field of infinite possibilities. You are one with all that exists – one with God. The infinite life force flows through you, expresses itself through you, and experiences life AS you. There is nothing apart from this infinite life force. It is All in All. The indivisible Whole is contained in each of the parts, and each of the parts is contained within the Whole. You lack nothing. God is the ground of your being, your own deepest nature. God is not just a being. **God is Being itself** – everywhere present and eternal. Infinite Being flows through *every* life form – every being. Relish this. Savor it. Laugh at the irony of it! You are already Whole. We are all One!

"We are already one. But we imagine that we are not. And what we have to recover is our original unity. What we have to be is what we are."

– Thomas Merton

PART II

LOVE'S EXPRESSION

Transforming what we know into who we are

Chapter 14

LOVE OF CREATING HARMONY

As we feel the love within us grow and expand to include our family, our associates, our community, and ultimately our universe, we are magically transformed from feeling incomplete to an emerging awareness of our intrinsic wholeness and worth. Our awakening inner spirit senses its oneness with all that is, and also recognizes its responsibility as a contributor to maintaining our harmony with all of nature. Suddenly, instead of trying to fill imagined ego-needs, we now want to express in some outward fashion the fullness of love we feel toward the whole gamut of life in the universe. Our cup runs over and we want to give back for all we have been given. We want to translate knowing into being, by bringing the fruits of our new knowledge into physical manifestation. By creating harmony and well-being in the world, we become the peacemakers and the nation builders.

Musically, *harmony* is defined as a combination of simultaneously sounding notes producing chords which have a pleasant effect. Where pockets of harmony exist in a community, there is accord, altruism, cooperation, compassion, compromise, and unanimous contributions to the good of the whole. Is this not *love in action*? Where dissonance and disharmony exist between individuals or nations, there is discord, greed, bias, friction, conflict, and people working against each other. This is nothing more than an *absence of love*. The culprit? Once again, it is the ego's disruptive force.

The ego desperately and unnecessarily tries to embellish itself, but only manages to further suppress its own undiscovered Divine nature. It is sad how we needlessly create our own misery when we remain trapped inside the confines of our ego.

Modern-day genius Ervin Laszlo first became famous as a child prodigy and concert pianist. At the age of five, he could hear a piece of music and then sit down and play it. At the age of fourteen, he was performing at Carnegie Hall. But the mathematical precision of the musical notes fascinated him and beckoned him to a deeper exploration of the perfection and harmony of the universe as a whole. This eventually led to his studies in quantum physics, system theories, cosmology, and philosophy. Because of that early love of harmony, he was able to integrate quantum science with ancient spiritual beliefs in a coherent system. Dr. Laszlo is now generally recognized as the founder of systems philosophy and general evolution theory.

What is the best way to express harmony in our own lives? One way is to listen closely to our self-talk. Are we telling ourselves that we are innately worthless or incapable? That we need to constantly compensate for the good we believe we lack? Or can we accurately affirm that we do have the Divine within us and, as such, are wholly complete and connected with the rest of humanity? When we allow our Divine essence to express *through* us, we are fully capable of creating the happiness and harmony to produce a satisfying life. Whenever a negative thought occurs, try replacing it with a positive counterpart. With some practice, you will begin to feel better, and you will also have a new tool for reprogramming any negative beliefs you have about yourself.

Another way to promote harmony is the art of listening to others. A psychologist once said that he had learned how to build very effective relationships with parents whose children he had just evaluated. Rather than initially unloading the examination results onto the parents, who were often already in a defensive posture, he would first ask, "I've seen your child for two hours, but you have lived with him for ten years. What are your principal concerns for your child? How do you see him?" At this point, the parents were in total harmony with the psychologist, proving that listening often "says" much more than talking does. It tells the speaker that you value his views and care about his feelings. Thus, a relationship of harmony and trust develops.

Another way to create harmony is to give from the heart. Albert Einstein once stated, "Only a life lived for others is a life worthwhile." Additionally, all major religions embrace a central principle of what we know as the Golden Rule, which is to "do unto others as you would have others do unto you." But what if you do not feel *worthy* of receiving? Just remember that part of giving is allowing others to experience the joy of giving to us. So receive with a grateful heart, because you are worthy of all good things! Try not to give with an expectation of receiving something in return. Some schools of thought view anonymous giving as the highest form of altruism. Others believe the greatest gift we can give to others is a Self-realized personhood. Giving from a pure heart gives rise to the richest harmony on every level.

Joy and laughter can create instant harmony. Laughter dispels tension where there was once stress and conflict. Norman Cousins once wrote of "laughing himself well" by viewing comedies and humorous productions from his hospital bed. People are instinctively drawn to individuals who have developed a degree of inner serenity and a contagious sense of humor. They understandably want what that joyful person has. Happy people are more social and enjoy more harmonious relationships. Happiness makes us attractive.

The foundation of our happiness lies in our thinking. As Charles Fillmore said, "Thoughts held in mind produce after their kind." Our thoughts beget feelings and actions. So, negative thoughts produce negative feelings and negative actions. When we believe that we are less than whole and are separated from our true Self, we are much more likely to create unhappiness. When we allow identification with our true and Divine Self, the way is opened for our natural joy to shine through.

Introduce some positive thoughts and pleasant changes into your life. Treat yourself to something new. Attend a comedy at your favorite theatre. Have some fun, and in the process bring some happiness and harmony into someone else's life. You are capable of completely dismantling the ego simply by opening your heart and expressing your love, light, and laughter.

"The habit of identifying with a mistaken sense of self and objective phenomena causes the illusion of confined existence. When this error in perception is corrected, our consciousness is immediately restored to its original, pure wholeness."
– Roy Eugene Davis

"It is only as we allow the Divine current to flow through us in and out, that we really express life."
– The Science of Mind

Chapter 15

LOVE OF CREATING BEAUTY

"All manifestation of Life is from an invisible to a visible plane, through a silent, effortless process of spiritual realization. We must unify our own mentalities with pure spirit."

– The Science of Mind

The philosopher Plato wrote a great deal about the ultimate values of Goodness, Truth, Justice, and Beauty. Beauty, he said, was an idea or form of which beautiful things were a consequence. This suggests that beauty might be an idealized concept of what constitutes perfection as it might be created or expressed in form. The dictionary defines beauty as "a characteristic of an animal, idea, object, person or place that provides a perceptual experience of pleasure or satisfaction." Other sources have called it: "A pleasing symmetry or balance perceived by the beholder"; "A manifestation of the Divine"; "A harmony of the soul that we achieve through cultivating feeling in a rational and tempered way." Some contemporary meanings you may have heard are "Beauty is in the eye of the beholder" and "Beauty is only skin deep," suggesting that it has nothing to do with character or integrity. All of this indicates the difficulty in finding a precise definition for beauty. We may only be able to evaluate what qualifies as beautiful to us when we experience it.

The moment we experience the Source of love within us, there is a profound change that comes over us, followed by a deep desire to express that love in some quantifiable fashion. It may take the form of philanthropy, art, music, literature, architecture, or the performing arts. But it always takes some form of creativity – gifts expressed from our true Self. When we reach this point, we no longer passively react to whatever life hands us. After recognizing the wholeness of our Divine essence, we instead take an active role as creators of our own destiny. As the quote above says, we manifest Life from an invisible to a visible plane. We convert ideas into reality. We transform what we *know* into who we *are*. Now *that* is beautiful!

> *"The most beautiful people we have known are those who have known defeat, known suffering, known struggle, known loss, and have found their way out of the depths. These persons have an appreciation, a sensitivity, and an understanding of life that fills them with compassion, gentleness, and a deep loving concern. Beautiful people do not just happen."*
>
> **– Elisabeth Kübler-Ross**

Chapter 16

LOVE OF EXPLORING THE MYSTERIES OF THE UNIVERSE

Countless frontiers still abound. As each is explored and understood, deeper mysteries emerge. Answering old questions gives birth to undiscovered new fields of study, which fans the thrill of uncovering new knowledge!

Oceans, Land, and Space. Seventy percent of our ocean depths remain unexplored. Scientists estimate that millions of new aquatic species are yet to be identified. Many rainforest land areas remain unexamined. The content of space consistently intrigues us with freshly reported sightings of new galaxies, planets, and moons. Most fascinating of all is the possibility of finding other life forms in other galaxies. Just who or what is out there?

Inventions. Man's miraculous inventions have helped us understand many of life's mysteries. Satellites, spaceships, and telescopes are addressing questions about the universe. We have indeed landed on the moon and Mars, but have we yet fully "landed on the earth" regarding issues of governments working in concert with each other?

Driverless cars are on the road. Current communication devices are remarkable, but they do not always produce a closer harmony between people. Machines alone are not the cure for the inclusion and coherence we seek.

Medical Science. Advances in medical treatments, surgery, and new medicines have been awe-inspiring – most particularly for those whose bodies have been healed and renewed. One day, given a persistent research offensive, certain stubborn cancers, Alzheimer's disorders, and other so-called "incurable" diseases will yield to treatment as well. The elimination of birth defects will equate to untold blessings. With sustained scientific advances, man's physical life will continue to be extended and enhanced.

The Mind of Man. Your mind holds the key to the comprehension that you are both complete and connected. We know that focusing thoughts in a systematic and positive way can dramatically improve physical disorders, as well as promote happiness and well-being. It just takes a persistent and concentrated effort. Those who yearn to understand more about the mysteries of our existence, including the nature of Ultimate Reality, will remain the perennial pioneers, explorers, and students of Life. They will search and search until at last they discover within the depths of their own being a Divine Self that is the source and sustainer of all that is. They then will become the innovators, inventors, and creators of Life, and they will realize that's what they have been all along!

"The answer to every question is within man, because man is within Spirit, and Spirit is an indivisible Whole!"
– The Science of Mind

Chapter 17

MAINTAINING THE BALANCE OF NATURE - THROUGH LOVE AND RESPECT FOR ALL LIFE FORMS, WITHOUT WHICH WE COULD NOT EXIST

Now and then, we come across an article about an ancient culture living in some remote part of the globe that has managed to live in complete harmony with nature and with each other right up to the present day. Their needs are simple, so their footprint on the earth is small. They are non-violent; they have maintained a love and respect for life in all its forms; and they experience a peace and contentment foreign to modern man. They live in a state of grace unknown to most people, and so we asked, "What happened? Why don't we live like this anymore?"

Here's why. Our "fall from grace" occurred when we began to believe in *duality*. We began to see ourselves as something *separate* and apart – from God, from others, and from nature. It was a false belief, but (in mythological terms) we ate from the Tree of the Knowledge of Good and Evil anyway. And thus began our symbolic exile from Paradise.

A few of these ancient cultures retained their belief in the unity of all things and continued to experience a feeling of oneness – with God, with others, and with nature. They kept a reverence for Life – in all its forms – and so did not feel separate from or superior to anything else. There was nothing to conquer because they were *part* of everything; they were instinctually *one* with all of nature.

We chose to leave the Garden of Eden behind when we chose to believe we were separate from the rest of the world. But we are *not* separate. When we destroy nature, we destroy a part of ourselves. When we go to war with each other, we are killing a part of ourselves. When we see God as separate, we see ourselves as separate from all that is sacred, and thus we are cutting ourselves off from our own spiritual Source, our deepest reality.

So, how do we solve this problem? How do we take personal responsibility for the *larger whole,* of which we are a part? How do we return to a state of grace? Can we go backward and live in harmony with nature like the animals of the forest? Or is the pristine Garden of Eden gone? In its place, we have created a world of polarity where we see everything in terms of opposites: black and white, good and evil, or to put it more bluntly, "what's good for me versus what's not good for me." This world of duality pits man against man, man against nature, and even man against himself. We have lost the deep sense of connection.

We no longer feel a sense of *belonging* or *oneness* with the infinite life force inherent in all things. We care more about our small individual self than we care about our universal Self. We have chosen to identify solely with matter at the expense of spirit.

And now, knowing this, the only way out is forward. We can no longer return to a state of *unconscious* union with the earth; we must go forward to a state of *conscious* oneness with the entire Cosmos. We must embody what we know. The world can no longer be our enemy, because quite literally we *are* the world.

We are each a part of the whole, whether we know it or not. The world is a unity. We are all connected in spirit – to God, to others, and to nature – and the connecting force is *love*. We must summon all of our courage and eat symbolically from the Tree of Life. It is the only way forward out of the maze of duality, where ego consciousness rules and strife triumphs. There is a higher level of consciousness available to us. Find the love within you, and love will show you the way.

Take personal stock today of your efforts on behalf of *your* larger body, Mother Earth. How are you protecting and nurturing her? Are you giving her body the same care you would give to your human body, or are you still stuck in a me-first mode of thinking? Are you recycling everything you can, or contributing more junk to a nearby landfill? Are you wasting precious resources such as water, paper, or trees? Are you doing your part to reduce conspicuous consumption? Are you polluting the air we breathe? Are you advocating and using renewable and sustainable energy sources as much as you possibly can? Do you have a solar panel? Does your house have adequate insulation to keep it warmer in the winter and cooler in the summer?

Your local conservation department will have many suggestions for doing your part. Contact them to learn more. As the international Charter for Compassion says, **"Think globally. Act locally."**

"All creation is unified in God's wholeness."
– Bhagavad Gita 11:5

"He who is plenteously provided for from within needs but little from without."

– Goethe

PART III

CONCLUSIONS

Chapter 18

LIVING LOVE

Allow unconditional love to triumph over competition,
division, and ego needs.

Enlightenment, according to the world's great wisdom teachers, is a total transformation of one's perception that results in a completely new worldview. It is not simply a scientific worldview, nor is it simply a religious worldview. Rather, it encompasses all of these in a broader spiritual worldview that sees life as a Whole. It results in a dramatic shift in one's understanding of ultimate reality, and brings profound peace and joy to the person who experiences it.

In that moment, one recognizes, unequivocally, that we are all eternally connected in consciousness as part of that larger universal Whole, and the fear of death melts away. A state of bliss and fulfillment replaces all fear, and the person is changed forever. They not only feel love; they *become* love. And they know that, in some inexplicable way, they ARE the world. They know that even though their material body appears to be only a limited *part* of the world, their higher Spirit is unlimited; it *is* the totality.

It is difficult to communicate this life-changing transformation in words and concepts to anyone who has not felt it. Yet the experience is more *real* than any level of consciousness they have ever experienced before. And the experience is becoming more and more common every single day. This state of Being is our evolutionary destiny.

Absent a life-transforming mystical experience such as this, we have tried to demonstrate that it is yet possible to gradually reprogram our thinking, uplift our perception of who we are, and overcome duality thinking. We have begun to understand what constitutes ultimate reality. By allowing our identity to steadily mature until it integrates every level of life into our sense of self, we've discovered we may be able to sneak up on enlightenment – the awakening realization of our true Self. And if this broader awareness also translates *knowing* into *being*, we can continue to evolve and benefit the earth and all of its life forms.

To remind us of their power, let us first briefly review our chapters. In addition to love of self, we have learned to love and appreciate our interconnection and interdependence with our family, the animals, nature, our institutions, our community, our country, people who are different, countries that are different, the earth, and the universe. We have presented evidence demonstrating that we could not exist without each of these. Hopefully, at each stage in the process, we've also allowed our identity to expand to include every level of life up to and including the universe, to which we are connected and to which we owe our survival. It would be tragic for our identity to remain at the small, stunted, ego-bound stage of our childhood.

But in case we haven't yet incorporated every segment of life into our identity of Oneness with the universe, let's consider the following questions.

1. Imagine your fate without your family, or some other human form of sustenance, during the time when you were at the vulnerable stage of newborn infant, toddler, or preschooler. Could you have survived without that human connection?

2. Could humanity have evolved to its present level of sophistication without animals? Could early humans have survived at all without the animals as a food source?

3. Without trees and plants, would humans have emerged as a species on planet Earth? Without soil and water, could human life have evolved on our planet?

4. Where would you be without places of learning, places of worship, social groups, workplaces, and recreational facilities? Without all of the institutions of modern civilization, where would the state of your existence be today?

5. Could you survive on your own, today, without the skills and contributions of those in your community who provide food, housing, clothing, medical care, protection under the law, transportation, education, and maintenance for us?

6. How much of your success do you owe to the freedom and the many opportunities you enjoy living in this country?

7. Do you have a reverence and appreciation for the many cultures and nations that came before us and discovered essentials such as fire, the wheel, spoken language, written language, spiritual revelations, and scientific inventions, which have all raised our consciousness and produced new ethical behaviors and new systems of government – even democracy itself?

8. Could you survive without the existence of Mother Earth? Without the beautiful harmony of the heavens with the earth, the sun, the moon, and the stars?

9. Have you yet realized the interconnectedness of ALL life in the universe? Have you realized you are a product of the evolution of the universe?

10. Have you experienced your infinite and Divine Spirit within, which connects every finite creation? Do you feel you are a part of the Whole? Or do you still identify with your ego's sense of being a separate entity? If so, go back and re-read the parable of the beautiful hand.

One person who practices the oneness of humanity is W. Kamau Bell with his groundbreaking interviews for the TV series *United Shades of America*. He humanizes the truism that if anyone is living in poverty, then a part of *ourselves* is living in poverty, because **we are all connected as one**. If we don't love a person in poverty, then we really don't love ourselves, because **we are all connected as one**. Everyone is a part of you, and you are a part of them. What we do unto others, we do unto *ourselves*. So, if you don't love a family member, or an animal, or nature, or institutions, or your community, or your country, or people who are different from you, or countries that are different from yours, or the earth, or the entire universe, then you don't fully love yourself, because **we are all connected as one**. It all starts with YOU!

Here is the bottom line: We could NOT survive without the rest of the universe! Our universe is an organic WHOLE, of which we are an undivided and essential part. If you believe you are *separate* from the Whole, you are suffering from a serious delusion – a delusion that will have dire consequences for your survival and the survival of all others on planet Earth…including the planet itself. To bury your head in the sand and foolishly consider only your individual ego's well-being, rather than the good of the Whole, of which you are a part, will inevitably lead to your extinction!

We cannot overstate the urgency of this necessary shift in perception or the consequences if we remain in ego consciousness. It is a question of evolve or perish. Live or die. Or more specifically, LOVE or die.

We must maintain the balance of nature, through love and respect for ALL life forms, without which we could not survive. We have a responsibility to the Whole, *because we are part of that Whole*! We challenge any one of you to try to survive without Mother Earth, the sun, the trees, the plants, the animals, and the millions of humans who contribute to YOUR welfare. Enlightenment is no longer a luxury; it's a *necessity*! Dear friends, the time is *now* to expand your awareness and discover who you really are!

It was part of humanity's childhood to believe we were nothing more than a material body. But it is time for us to grow up now, to the good news that we are more than that, SO MUCH MORE! Ego consciousness must yield to a higher, happier, more evolved level of consciousness that has the hope and the promise to bring about peace and harmony among humans and nations before it's too late.

IF we can realize that we are literally all part of each other, we might have a chance to overcome the greed, hatred, and discrimination so prevalent today toward people we believe to be "others."

IF we can realize we are killing a part of *ourselves* when we take a life – any life – we might learn respect, tolerance, acceptance, and yes, LOVE for each other.

"Love your neighbor as yourself" was the prophetic directive issued over 2,000 years ago. Today, we learn that your neighbor **IS** your Self! Move beyond your narrow, superficial ego belief in separation for your own sake, as well as for others. What joy awaits you when you do!

And if you have been taught from an early age to believe that you are innately imperfect or that you were born into a state of original sin, we implore you to find the courage to examine these false beliefs and move beyond them! No one should be allowed to teach you that you came into this world to hate yourself or to feel inadequate or inferior. You are a whole, complete, and beautiful child of God, united in a shared universal and Divine consciousness. No one should ever convince you otherwise. Believe in yourself. Trust your highest instincts. Love yourself. Love ALL of life, the environment, the planet, and the cosmos. Maintain a reverence for Life in its entirety, because it is all Divine in its essential nature. We are Whole. We are One.

"Come out of the circle of time and into the circle of love."
– Rumi

"He who is filled with love is filled with God himself."
– St. Augustine

EPILOGUE

Feeling the Love

How will you know when your ego is in the rearview mirror and you have moved into a higher level of consciousness? Is there a way to recognize your "Divine Self"? How will you know when you are functioning from your true Self, rather than your ego-self? Even though your Divine essence is invisible, you will know when you are living in it, because you will feel the following:

1. You will feel a joy in giving – of your time, your talent, your love and concern.

2. You will feel abundant, as if you are overflowing with love – more than you alone need, and you will feel moved to share it with others. It will radiate out of you to such a degree that it can be experienced by those around you.

3. You will feel whole and complete, as if there is not a single thing in the entire universe that you need. You will feel contentment, comfort, and peace.

4. You will feel a sense of oneness – a knowing that your spirit is connected with everything – all life forms, the universe, God. No one you meet will feel like a stranger to you because of that deep connection.

5. Your creativity will be enlivened, as Infinite Love begins to express through you, whether in the form of the arts, the building trades, creative cooking, music, or something else. You become a creator whose love is made manifest.

6. You will feel a sense of freedom as you are lifted out of the heaviness of your ego-self and into the lightness of your Divine-Self. Work suddenly feels effortless. Life feels carefree.

7. You will care about the well-being of the Whole, because you are a part of it.

8. Your fear of death will dissolve as you realize physical death does not extinguish your essential Being.

9. Your interest in materialism, wealth, and power will decrease as your compassion, generosity, and altruism increase.

10. You will see your Self in others, and others in your Self.

Let us conclude with a beautiful quote from Neale Donald Walsch:

> *I believe God wants you to know ... that **love** is not what you want; it is what you **are**. It is very important to not get these two confused.*
>
> *If you think that love is what you want, you will go*

searching for it all over the world. If you think love is what you are, you will go sharing it all over the place. The second approach will cause you to find what the searching will never reveal.

Yet, you cannot give love in order to get it. Doing that is as much as saying you do not now have it.

And that statement will, of course, be your reality. No, you must give love because you have *it to give. In this you will experience your own possession of it.*

GLOSSARY

Definitions as used in this book

A

A BEING. An individual finite manifestation of the infinite life force – of BEING ITSELF. (Example: a single human being.)

ASCEND. Move to a higher level of perception or understanding.

AWAKENING. Expanding one's conscious awareness to the presence of a higher level of reality.

AWARENESS. To increasingly realize, be sensitive to, and have knowledge of one's thoughts, feelings, emotions, and behaviors in all life situations. Basic consciousness; cognizance; sentience; mindfulness; ability to perceive or discern.

B

BEAUTY. A quality of the soul that gives pleasure or deep satisfaction to the senses or the mind; a work of art.

BEING ITSELF. The formless, infinite life force or energy throughout the entire universe. (Example: the One Infinite Life Force within each and every finite being.)

BELIEF. Conviction held in the mind, or confidence in the truth or existence of something not immediately susceptible to rigorous proof.

C

CONNECTED. United, linked, or joined. Associated in a relationship.

CONSCIOUS. Aware of one's own existence, thoughts, and surroundings. Known to oneself. Not automatic, instinctual, or the result of conditioning; deliberate or intentional activity of the mind. Awake to an inner realization of a fact, truth, or condition.

CONSCIOUSNESS. Awareness. Thoughts and feelings, collectively, of an individual or of an aggregate of people. Full activity of the mind; knowing. A field of infinite possibilities. A source of unlimited creativity.

COSMIC CONSCIOUSNESS. Universal awareness. A field of infinite possibilities. A source of unlimited creativity. Level of consciousness higher than the ego.

COSMOS. The world or universe regarded as an orderly, harmonious system. Form.

CREATIVITY. Ability to bring something new or unique into being from originality of thought or expression; gifts expressed from our true Self.

D

DEFINE. To limit or explain. To delineate, portray, or outline in thought or words.

DIVINE. Godlike characteristic or spiritual aspect; having qualities attributed to a god; e.g., goodness, creativity; immortality.

DIVINE SELF. One's highest level of consciousness. True Self. Operating in universal consciousness, the field of all possibilities.

DUALITY. Divided into two opposing substances or principles, such as mind and matter, or good and evil. Belief in separation; e.g., God is "up there" and we are "down here."

E

EGO. A projected self-image or sense of self created by identifying exclusively with form (i.e., the physical body, the brain, thoughts, feelings, actions, and material things). Ego sees the self as a separate finite thing that is imperfect, limited, and lacking. As a result, it will create a self-image of inferiority or superiority, based on its belief in need, fear, and protection. False self.

EGO-SELF. A restricted level of consciousness which endeavors to protect or enhance one's physical being by creating a pseudo façade to either appease the self or to project to others. False self. Self-image.

ENLIGHTENMENT. A total transformation of one's perception that results in a radical change in worldview; a paradigm shift in one's understanding of ultimate reality; alteration in our perspective on life as a whole.

ESSENCE. Your core Being; your Divine inner spirit; your connection with cosmic or universal consciousness. Your Divine essence is whole, complete, without needs, and connected to all that is; it is your True Self.

EVIL. Absence of good; absence of love.

F

FINITE. Having bounds or limits. Measurable. Not infinite or infinitesimal. Not zero. Subject to conditions of space, time, and laws of nature.

FORGIVENESS. To cease feeling resentment toward another. To let go and transcend negative feelings associated with the perceived transgressions of another.

FORM. Finite matter. Usually has mass or volume. Everything found in the material universe; within space/ time. Includes the physical body, the brain, thoughts, feelings, ideas, actions, and physical things. May be created in the mind or in physical matter. Usually perceived as a separate thing.

FORMLESS. Lacking a definite form or shape. Invisible and indefinable. Unbounded.

FREE WILL. Free choice. Unrestricted voluntary decision.

G

GIVING. To voluntarily provide or bestow or present. Contribute generously. Donate.

GOD. Unlimited, formless, all-inclusive Being. Field of all possibilities. Infinite life force or energy; capable of expressing or manifesting as finite form, without being limited by it.

GOOD. Full of love. Beneficial, pleasant, agreeable, moral excellence, virtue, benevolent, humane, kind, essence, the best part of anything.

GRACE. Goodwill. The freely given love of God. A virtue or excellence of Divine origin. The influence or spirit of God operating in man. Moral strength. Kindness.

H

HARMONY. Accord, altruism, cooperation, compassion, compromise, and unanimous contributions to the good of the whole. Concord, unity, blending peacefully. Love in action.

HEART. Center of the total personality. The innermost or central part of anything. A vital or essential part; core.

HEAVEN/PARADISE. A state of mind. A state of supreme happiness, wholeness, and oneness that is experienced as a result of awakening to our Divine nature.

HELL. A state of mind. A state of torment or misery that is self-created by the "separate" ego.

HOME. A feeling of inner security and peace; an inner haven of stability, strength, clarity, purpose, and creative potential; a sense of belonging.

I

IDENTITY. Who or what you believe you are at any given moment. May reflect a self-image created by the ego or a true identity based on knowledge of your Divine essence.

INCOMPLETE. A feeling of being flawed or limited in some aspect. Lacking some part.

INFINITE. Unbounded, unlimited, perfect. Endless, innumerable; inexhaustible. Immeasurably, indefinitely, or exceedingly great. Infinite Being or God.

INTENTION. The act of firmly fixing thoughts and emotions upon some planned action or potential result. The resolve or determination to follow through with its manifestation.

J

JUDGMENT. The forming of an opinion, estimate, notion, or conclusion from circumstances presented to the mind. A determination or opinion formed. A discernment or discrimination. A verdict.

K

L

LEVEL OF CONSCIOUSNESS. Visualize levels of consciousness as ever-expanding concentric circles through which we pass, from smallest to largest, during our evolution. Animal past = instinctual. Human present = ego/self-conscious. Spiritual future = the Whole.

LOVE. A feeling of oneness, connectedness; a sense of unity with others, with nature, with God. Expressing affection, care, and concern for the object of one's love; identification with what is other than self. Divine attribute of connection and unity with all of life. Charity. Deep and enduring regard.

M

MANIFESTING. To materialize or bring into being as a result of one's thoughts, intentions, and behaviors.

MIND. Intelligence or intellectual power; capacity to generate thoughts. Mind is a property of universal consciousness, not of the brain.

N

NEED. Lack of something wanted or perceived as necessary; feeling of being incomplete as you presently are.

O

ONENESS. A spiritual connection; a state of unity with universal energy; connected as a single unit.

P

PARABLE. A short allegorical story designed to convey a truth or moral lesson. It conveys a meaning indirectly by the use of comparison or analogy.

PEACE. Freedom from anxiety or mental disturbance. A state of tranquility and serenity; stillness.

Q

R

S

SELF. The subject of experience, as contrasted with the object of experience. For example: the seer as opposed to what is seen. Contains both wholeness and oneness within its Divine essence, whether that is consciously known or not. For purposes of this book, lowercase self symbolizes ego self, and uppercase Self symbolizes Divine Self.

SELF-ESTEEM. Respect for or a favorable impression of oneself. Pride.

SELF-IMAGE. The idea, conception, or mental image one has of oneself.

SELF-LOVE. Awareness and acceptance of your eternal value and worth exactly the way you are. Self-respect. A feeling of well-being.

SEPARATE. Kept apart by an intervening barrier or space. Existing independently. Split, severed, disconnected, divided, detached, or disjoined.

SPIRIT. Soul. Within the individual, the aspect of the Divine that is connected with the Whole.

STABILITY. The ability of an object to maintain or restore equilibrium when acted upon by forces tending to displace it. Strength. Permanence within, despite changes without. Ability to remain centered and calm within your Divine Self. Analogy: the eye of the hurricane.

SURRENDER. Letting go or giving over one's energies to the loving forces of the universe. Openness, trust, and receptivity to the influences of higher levels of consciousness.

T

THE WHOLE. The Infinite. Universal Divinity. God. Being itself, which contains all finite beings. All-in-All.

TRUTH. A verified or indisputable fact, proposition, or principle.

U

UNCONDITIONAL LOVE. Love not limited by conditions. Complete, unqualified love. Absolute love.

UNCONSCIOUS. Not known to the conscious mind. Automatic, instinctual, or conditioned thoughts or actions that are below the level of the conscious awareness.

UNITY. In unison with all creation; oneness. Seeing no distinction between perception of the Self and others. A single whole encompassing all parts. Connectedness.

UNIVERSAL. Metaphysical entity that remains unchanged in character within a series of external changes or changing relations. Characteristic of all or the Whole. Existing everywhere.

UNIVERSALITY. Existence or prevalence everywhere.

UNIVERSE. The totality of known objects and phenomena throughout space and time. The cosmos; macrocosm. The whole world in which everything exists. A manifestation of infinite Being.

V

W

WHOLENESS. Full; complete; without diminution; total; undivided; integral; unbroken; intact; a unitary system; undiminished; totality; the entirety.

X, Y, Z

ABOUT THE AUTHORS

Sandy Meadows

Sandy Meadows is a freelance writer, published author, and philosopher (lover of wisdom) with a lifelong passion to understand the nature of ultimate reality. Over the years, she has published poetry, essays, and articles in various magazines and literary journals. She has worked in corporate communications, investor relations, office management, and has been an executive assistant to several corporate presidents. She serves on the board of

Compassionate Indy, which is part of the international Charter for Compassion movement dedicated to making the world a more compassionate place. She resides in Avon, Indiana, and her two children and three grandchildren live nearby.

Sandy's first book, *The Great Comforter*, details a life-transforming mystical experience that radically altered her worldview about what constitutes reality, life, death, God, and man. She states it was like a quantum leap into a higher level of consciousness, where everything was connected in an infinite continuum and nothing was separate. All fear of death was erased. While in that state of higher consciousness, she experienced the divinity and oneness of all life forms, connected as a single Whole of Being. And for the first time in her life, all the pieces of life's puzzle began to fit together. She realized that if we are all One, the only real moral imperative is to love and care for the well-being of the Whole, of which we are a part. She realized that if everything is part of what we call "God," then *everything* has infinite value.

These insights so enriched her life and her relationships that she wanted to put the principles into practice and share them with others. Sandy considered them too important *not* to share, because she knew that everything we do in part affects the Whole. She felt that this new level of consciousness was destined to be part of our collective evolution. Thus, it became part of her life's purpose to share with others what she had learned during that mystical experience. Dr. Wenck's interest in sharing knowledge of this same worldview resulted in a perfect collaboration, and *Love or Die* was the result.

Email address for the author: indianawriter@sbcglobal.net

Stan Wenck, Ed.D.

Stan Wenck, Ed.D., is a practicing clinical psychologist and professor emeritus of psychology following thirty-one years of teaching at Ball State University in Muncie, Indiana. He is licensed both as a health service provider in psychology and school psychologist in Indiana. Love or Die serves as his 80th authored or co-authored publication. Recent books by Dr. Wenck include Train Your Brain to Get Happy as well as Love Him, Love His Kids! targeting stepmothers-to-be. Still in frequent use is his graduate text, House-Tree-Person Drawings: An Illustrated Diagnostic Manual, first printed in 1978 and used in building a personality "picture" by analysis of a subject's drawings.

Dr. Wenck's teaching specialties included various psycho-diagnostics with children and adults as well as personality development. He has developed and taught courses involving the training of clinicians in using biofeedback therapies in the treatment of various psychophysiological disorders. Additionally, by employing techniques of guided imagery and visualization, certain of his clients have achieved dramatic remissions from disease entities, including psoriasis and certain malignancies.

Some eight years ago, Dr. Wenck became interested in the study of various aspects of spiritual thought – principally those which foster the idea that, rather than being afflicted with so-called original sin, humans are blessed with a godly divinity within each of us that should be acknowledged, embraced, and manifested for the good of oneself and others. He feels that this notion has transformed his therapeutic approach and effectiveness with his patients. His current aim is that of empowering clients to discover, develop, and expand their inner divinity and talents. "As a result," he reveals, "my client relationships have become more enriched," and adds, "Clients now seem eager to enter their counseling sessions and frequently appear at the door asking, 'May I be next?'" He finds that the adoption of these principles has added a significant degree of joy and authenticity in his personal relationships as well. Additionally, he experiences a feeling of liberation from conditioned societal pressures and resulting life expectations.

The above circumstances prompted Dr. Wenck to welcome an invitation from Sandy Meadows to co-author *Love or Die* in order to publicly share and promote the concepts of our individual divinity, wholeness, and connection with all that is. He states, "Sandy's extraordinary experience serves as an inspirational example to each of us on our journey to becoming who we truly are." Dr. Wenck practices clinically at the Hopewell Center in Anderson, Indiana. He makes his home in Fishers, Indiana, and regularly attends and contributes to several spiritual book discussion groups in that vicinity.

ACKNOWLEDGEMENTS

To Larry Dossey, MD, our deep gratitude for the generous statement of encouragement and counsel he offered in support of our manuscript. Thank you for your enduring confidence in us!

To Philip Gulley, our thanks for his suggestion for the subtitle to our book, and the many other suggestions he offered which we believe will augment the success of *Love or Die*.

To Vince Lisi, our appreciation for the in-depth review and feedback on our original draft.

Thanks also to JoAnne Waeltz and the many friends and relatives who offered positive suggestions for expanding our text in ways that would benefit the reader's understanding of our message.

We love all of you.

RECOMMENDED READING

Adyashanti. The End of Your World. Boulder, CO: Sounds True, 2010.

Bruce, Robert. Energy Work: The Secrets of Healing and Spiritual Growth. Charlottesville, VA: Hampton Roads Publishing Company, 2011.

Butterworth, Eric. Discover the Power Within You: A Guide to the Unexplored Depths Within. New York, Harper Collins, 1989.

Chopra, Deepak. The Way of the Wizard. New York: Harmony Books, 1995

Dalai Lama and Desmond Tutu. The Book of Joy. New York: Avery, 2016.

Dispenza, Dr. Joe. Becoming Supernatural: How Common People Are Doing the Uncommon. Hay House Inc., 2017.

Dossey, Larry, M.D. One Mind: How Our Individual Mind is Part of a Greater Consciousness and Why It Matters. Hay House, Inc., 2013

Emoto, Masaru. The True Power of Water. Hillsboro, OR: Beyond Words Publishing, Inc., 2005

Gulley, Philip and James Mulholland. If God is Love. New York: Harper Collins Publishers, 2004

Hicks, Esther and Jerry Hicks. The Vortex. Carlsbad, CA: Hay House, Inc., 2009

Johnson, Lynn D., PhD. Enjoy Life: Healing with Happiness. Salt Lake City, UT: Head Acre Press, 2008

Lipton, Bruce H., Ph.D. and Steve Bhaerman. Spontaneous Evolution: Our Positive Future and a Way to Get There From Here. Hay House, Inc. 2009

Martin, Angela. Practical Intuition. New York: Barnes and Noble Books, 2002

Moorjani, Anita. Dying to Be Me. Carlsbad, CA: Hay House Inc., 2012

Ortberg, John. The Life You've Always Wanted. Grand Rapids, MI: Zondervan, 2002.

Pond, David. Chakras for Beginners. Woodbury, MN: Llewellyn Publications, 2008

Singer, Michael. The Untethered Soul: The Journey Beyond Yourself, New Harbinger Publications, Inc. 2007

Taylor, Steve. The Leap: The Psychology of Spiritual Awakening, New World Library, 2017.

Tolle, Eckhart and Patrick McDonnell. Guardians of Being. Navoto, CA: New World Library, 2009

Van Praagh, James. Talking to Heaven. New York: Harper Collins Publishers, 2004.

Zukav, Gary. Soul Stories. New York: Simon & Shuster, 2000.

CPSIA information can be obtained
at www.ICGtesting.com
Printed in the USA
FFHW021825070119
50099277-54942FF

9 781457 567131